PROPERTY OF
THE MONTCLAIR COOPERATIVE SCHOOL

How We Use

Water

Carol Ballard

Chicago, Illinois

© 2005 Raintree
Published by Raintree,
a division of Reed Elsevier, Inc.
Chicago, IL

All rights reserved. No part of this publication
may be reproduced or transmitted in any form or
by any means, electronic or mechanical, including
photography, recording, taping, or any information
storage and retrieval system, without permission
in writing from the publishers.

For information, address the publisher:
Raintree
100 N. LaSalle, Suite 1200
Chicago, IL 60602

Originated by Ambassador Litho
Printed and bound in China by
South China Printing Company

09 08 07 06 05
10 9 8 7 6 5 4 3 2 1

**Library of Congress Cataloging-in-
Publication Data**
Ballard, Carol.
  How we use water / Carol Ballard.
     p. cm. -- (Using materials)
  Includes bibliographical references and index.
  ISBN 1-4109-0607-8 -- ISBN 1-4109-0898-4
  1. Water--Juvenile literature. I. Title. II. Series.
  GB662.3.B36 2005
  533.7--dc22
                                          2004002921

Acknowledgments
The publisher would like to thank the following
for permission to reproduce photographs: p. 4
NASA; pp. 5 (Rod Planck), 6, 7 (Colin Cuthbert),
27 (Gilbert S. Grant) Science Photo Library; pp. 8
(OKAPIA), 11 (Andrew Plumptre), 16 (Gordon
Maclean), 28 (Doug Allan) Oxford Scientific
Films; pp. 9 (Stone), 10 (Photodisc/Harcourt
Index), 17 (TIB), 20 (Photodisc/Harcourt Index),
21 (Taxi), 22 (Photodisc/Harcourt Index), 23
(Imagebank), 24 (Thinkstock), 25, 26 (Photodisc/
Harcourt Index), 29 (Imagebank) Getty Images;
p. 12 photographersdirect.com; p. 13 Alamy;
p. 14 photolibrary.com; p. 15 (Harcourt Index)
Photodisc; p. 18 Robert Harding Picture Library;
p. 19 (Harcourt Index) Corbis.

Cover photograph of melting ice cubes
reproduced with permission of Zefa.

Every effort has been made to contact copyright
holders of any material reproduced in this book.
Any omissions will be rectified in subsequent
printings if notice is given to the publishers.

Contents

Some words are shown in bold, **like this.** You can find out what they mean by looking in the glossary.

Water and Its Properties

All the things we use are made from **materials.** Water is a material. Most of Earth is covered by water. It is in the air around us. It is needed by every living thing. Without it Earth would be a dry, dusty, dead place.

We use water every day for drinking, cooking, and washing. Water helps plants to grow. Ships travel on water, carrying people and goods to different places. Water is also used to provide power and **energy.**

Earth's oceans are easily seen from space.

Rain helps plants to grow.

The **properties** of a material tell us what it is like. One property of water is that it is colorless. It is also **transparent** and **odorless.** At normal **temperatures** water is a **liquid,** but it can also be a **solid** or a **gas.**

Do not use it!

The different properties of materials make them useful for some jobs. The properties also make them not as useful for other jobs. For example, we do not use water instead of gas in our cars. Water does not burn. So it would not give the car the energy it needs.

Where Does Water Come From?

Water is a **natural material.** About seven-tenths of Earth's surface is covered in water. All of our oceans, rivers, lakes, and puddles contain water. The ice at the North and South poles is frozen water.

Some reservoirs are natural lakes, but others are made by people.

Water is carried under the ground in pipes like these.

When we turn on a faucet, water comes out. It has had a long trip to get there. The trip begins when water flows into large lakes or **reservoirs.** The water is then cleaned at a water treatment plant. Dirt and **germs** are taken out. When the water is clean, it is stored in large tanks. Underground pipes carry water from the tanks to faucets in homes and schools.

Solid, liquid, or gas?

*We usually think of water as a clear **liquid.** But water can also be a **gas** or a **solid.** If you heat water to 212° Fahrenheit (100° Celsius), it boils and **evaporates.** It becomes a gas that we call **water vapor.** If you cool water to 32° Fahrenheit (0° Celsius), it freezes and becomes solid ice.*

The Water Cycle

Water is being **recycled** all the time. Warmth from the Sun heats the water in seas and lakes. This makes the water **evaporate. Water vapor** rises high into the air. The air is colder higher up. This cools the water vapor down and turns it back into tiny drops of **liquid** water. These drops join together to form clouds. The clouds are blown along by the wind. The drops then fall to the ground as rain or snow.

A snowflake is made from crystals of frozen water.

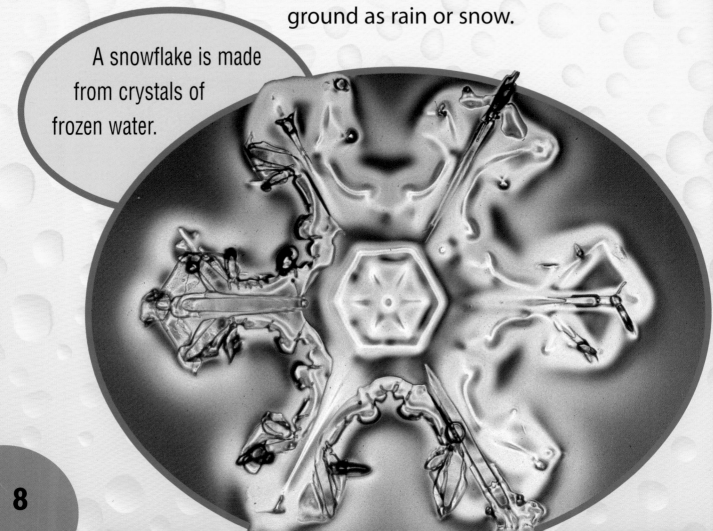

Some rivers bend and twist on their route to the sea.

This water comes together to form tiny streams. Small streams join to form larger streams and rivers. These streams and rivers flow into lakes and seas. There, the whole process starts all over again. This process is called the water cycle.

Breathing out

If you breathe out on a cold morning, your breath might look cloudy. This is because your breath is warm and contains water vapor. As the cold air cools your breath, the water vapor turns into tiny drops of liquid water.

Water for Drinking

About three-quarters of people's bodies is made from water. We need water to stay alive. People who go without water for several days can become very sick. Running, cycling, or dancing can make you hot and sticky. Your body loses water as you sweat. It is important to drink plenty of water to replace what you lose.

A glass of cold water is very refreshing on a hot day.

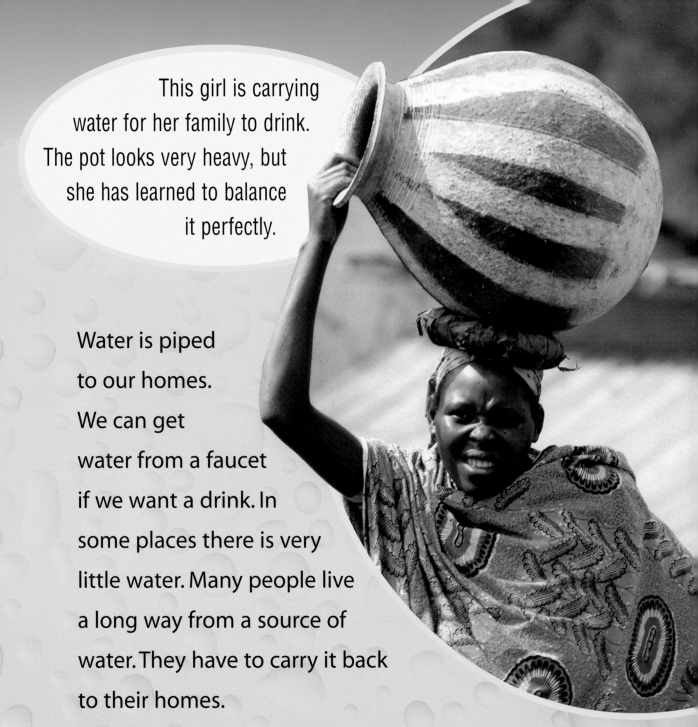

This girl is carrying water for her family to drink. The pot looks very heavy, but she has learned to balance it perfectly.

Water is piped to our homes. We can get water from a faucet if we want a drink. In some places there is very little water. Many people live a long way from a source of water. They have to carry it back to their homes.

Do not use it!

*Sweet, fizzy drinks contain water, but they often contain other things that are not good for you. Some have a lot of sugar that can hurt your teeth. Some have other **chemicals** in them. It makes sense not to drink too many of these drinks.*

Water for Washing

To stay clean we need to wash ourselves and the things that we use. Water is a good **material** to use for washing. This is because it is a **liquid** that does not harm our bodies. It washes dirt from our bodies and from things like dirty dishes. Water is colorless and also **odorless,** so we do not smell after we wash in it. Using soap can make things even cleaner.

Keeping clean can be fun, too!

A dry, breezy, sunny day is best for drying laundry.

When our clothes get dirty, they need to be washed. This can be done using a washing machine. Some fabrics are **delicate.** They need to be washed by hand. Plates, silverware, and saucepans all need to be washed after a meal. You can use a dishwasher or wash them by hand.

Do not use it!

Some types of cloth can be damaged if they get wet, so we do not use water to wash them. Dry cleaning uses special **chemicals** *instead of water to remove dirt. The chemicals clean the fabric. But they do not damage it.*

Cars can be washed using a bucket and sponge and a hose. Many service stations have machines that do the work for you.

Water for Playing

Almost everyone likes playing in water! We can float in water. We can jump into it without hurting ourselves. It is a good idea to learn to swim as soon as you can. This will help you stay safe in and around water. Swimming pools are good places to improve your swimming skills.

Before you swim, check how deep the water is and look for the lifeguard.

These two children are learning how to paddle a canoe.

Snorkeling lets you see what is happening underwater. Scuba divers can explore very deep water. Water sports such as windsurfing, sailing, and canoeing are all fun, too.

Taking a trip on a boat can be a good way to travel and look at the scenery. Cruise vacations on the sea or along rivers are popular.

Stay safe

Playing in water is fun. But it can also be dangerous. You must remember to be careful. Always obey the safety rules at a swimming pool, and read warning signs at beaches. Never swim on your own, and only use those places that are meant for water sports.

Water for Growing

All living things need water.
Plants need water to grow.
Most plants have roots
that hold them firmly in
the soil. Among other
things, the roots
absorb water from
the soil and carry it
to the other parts
of the plant.

Potted plants often need to
be watered every day in hot,
dry weather.

Plants that grow in hot, dry places need to save as much water as possible.

Farmers need to water large fields of crops. They use water pipes with pumps and sprinklers attached. These can spray water over entire fields.

Desert plants

Deserts are very dry places. Anything living there has to be able to survive with very little water. The thick stems of cacti store water, and their roots spread out just below the ground. This lets them absorb any water that falls.

Moving Water

Because water is a **liquid,** it can be poured. Wherever you put water, it will spread out to take the shape of its container. Water always flows downhill. It flows in a gentle trickle in a small mountain stream. But in large rivers, there is often a strong **force** called a **current.**

The force of these waves is enough to wear away the rocky cliffs.

The energy in moving water keeps a surfer on his board.

The movement of water downhill creates a force. We can use the force of moving water in many ways to create **energy.**

Tides

The water in seas and oceans is not still. Winds and currents make water rise and fall in waves. Waves can be small and gentle or strong and wild. Twice a day, the water in seas and oceans creeps closer to the shore. Twice a day it slips back away from the shore. These movements are called tides.

Water for Energy

People have used water to make things work for thousands of years. Water mills have large waterwheels. The **energy** in moving water turns a waterwheel. This then turns other wheels, which can pump water or work machines.

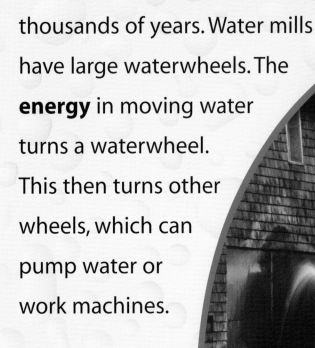

Water mills like this had many uses, including grinding grain for making bread.

Steam engines were used to pull trains carrying people and goods.

Water can be used to make electricity. Dams are built on rivers to hold water back. When water is let through, it flows downhill to a power plant. There, it turns wheels called **turbines.** These then turn **generators** that make electricity. The movement of tides and waves can be used in the same way.

Steam engines

*Steam engines can be used to power many machines. If water is heated, it boils and turns into a gas called **water vapor.** Water vapor needs more space than **liquid** water and will push on its container. This **force** can push a slide called a **piston** outward. The piston slides back in when the steam escapes. This action can make other parts move and turn.*

Water for Transportation

Water can be used to move things from one place to another. Some **materials** can float on water. Boats float because they are lighter than the water that would fill the same space. People have used boats for many thousands of years.

Cargo ships carry large, heavy goods around the world.

Cruise ships take travelers all over the world.

Small boats can carry people and goods on calm water such as rivers. Larger boats are needed to travel across rough seas and oceans. These boats carry passengers and goods around the world.

Canals are waterways made by people. They were built so boats could travel where there are no rivers. Today we have highways, railways, and airplanes. But the heaviest loads can still be carried on water.

Moving logs

When trees are cut down, they have to be moved to factories and paper mills. The logs are very heavy and difficult to move. In many places, they are pulled to a river and tied together to make a raft. This can then be floated on the water and guided downstream to wherever the logs are needed.

Water for Cooling

On a hot day, splashing cold water over ourselves is a great way to cool off. One **property** of water is that it can **absorb** heat but still feel cool. Water also does not **conduct** heat well. Car engines and machines in factories can be cooled down using cold water. Adding ice cubes to a **liquid** will cool the liquid down.

Popsicles are made by freezing water that contains **flavorings.**

Firefighters are trained to put out big fires like this one.

A fire needs heat to start. If heat is removed from a burning fire, the fire will go out. Putting water on a fire lowers the **temperature** enough to put it out. Firefighters often use water to put out big fires.

Do not use it!

Putting water on some fires can be dangerous. NEVER put water on burning grease or oil. Water and oil do not mix, and the fire will spread further. NEVER put water on an electrical fire. Water can conduct electricity, and you could get a dangerous electric shock.

Things That Live in Water

Water is home to many plants and creatures. Seas and oceans contain saltwater, but most rivers, lakes, and streams contain freshwater. Some living things can live only in saltwater while others can live only in freshwater.

Fish spend all their time in water. They use their **gills** to get oxygen from the water. Their fins and tails help them to swim.

Coral reefs give shelter to fish and other small creatures.

Jellyfish use their tentacles to sting their prey.

Animals such as frogs lay their eggs in water. These eggs hatch into tadpoles that will grow into adult frogs. When they are fully grown, they move onto land. Other animals, such as turtles, move easily between land and water. They can only breathe air, so they need to come to the water's surface often.

Breathing underwater

Humans cannot live in water. We can only breathe air. If we stay underwater too long, our lungs fill with water and we drown. When divers go underwater, they have to take air in special tanks on their backs.

Water and the Environment

Water controls where animals and plants can live. It also affects people's lives. Too much or too little rain can cause many problems. If too much rain falls in a short time, rivers may overflow. Water spills onto the land and ruins crops. Buildings can be damaged, and people may be left homeless.

In some countries, rain may not fall for many months. During **droughts,** crops become weak and die. Animals and people run out of food. Without emergency help, they may starve.

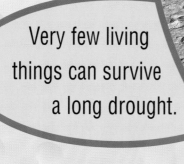

Very few living things can survive a long drought.

Most animals and plants cannot survive in polluted water like this.

Water may become **polluted** if people are careless with oil, dirt, **chemicals,** and garbage. These things can harm everything that lives in the water. Cleaning polluted water can take a long time and be very expensive.

Controlling floods

*Some rivers **flood** often, so people must be prepared. Dams have been built to control the floodwater. In other places, **flood barriers** have been built. Dams and barriers stop floods, but they may affect animals and plants that live in the rivers.*

Find Out for Yourself

The best way to find out more about water is to investigate it for yourself. Look around your home to see how water is being used, and keep an eye out for water during your day. You will find the answers to many of your questions in this book. You can also look in other books and on the Internet.

Books to read

Ballard, Carol. *Science Answers: Grouping Materials.* Chicago: Heinemann Library, 2003.
Burgan, Michael. *Land and Water.* Milwaukee, Wis.: Gareth Stevens, 2004.

Graham, Ian. *Water: A Resource Our World Depends On.* Chicago: Heinemann Library, 2004.

Hunter, Rebecca. *Discovering Science: Matter.* Chicago: Raintree, 2003.

Stewart, Melissa. *The Wonders of Water.* Minneapolis, Minn.: Compass Point Books, 2004.

Pancella, Peggy. *Water Safety.* Chicago: Heinemann Library, 2004.

Petersen, Christine. *Water Power.* Danbury, Conn.: Scholastic Library, 2004.

Stefanow, Jennifer. *Polluted Water.* Chicago: Raintree, 2004.

Using the Internet

Explore the Internet to find out more about water. Have an adult help you use a search engine. Type in keywords such as *water cycle, drought,* and *flood.*

Glossary

absorb soak up

chemical substance that we use to make other substances, or for jobs such as cleaning

conduct carry heat or electricity

current flow of something, for example, a river

delicate easily damaged

desert place where there is very little rain

drought long period of time with no rainfall

energy power to do work

evaporate when liquid water turns into a gas called water vapor

flavoring something added to a food or drink to give it a certain taste

flood water spilling over land

flood barrier wall or something else put up to stop floodwater from coming onto land

force push or a pull

gas something, like air, that spreads out into all the space it can

generator part of a power plant that makes electricity

germ tiny living thing that can make you sick

gill part of a fish's body that takes oxygen from water

liquid something that flows and can be poured from one container to another

material matter that things are made from

natural anything that is not made by people

odorless has no smell

piston part of an engine

polluted spoiled, dirty, or impure

property characteristic or quality of a material

recycle use again

reservoir lake for storing water

snorkel tube that lets you breathe as you swim underwater

solid having a certain shape and size

steam engine engine that is powered by steam that is made by boiling water

temperature measure of how hot or cold something is

transparent able to be clearly seen through

turbine part of the machinery at a power plant

water vapor water in the form of a gas; water turns into water vapor when it boils and evaporates

Index